X

My Apple

For a free color catalog describing Gareth Stevens' list of high-quality books, call 1-800-542-2595 (USA) or 1-800-461-9120 (Canada). Gareth Stevens' Fax: (414) 225-0377.

Library of Congress Cataloging-in-Publication Data

Davies, Kay.
    My apple / by Kay Davies and Wendy Oldfield; photographs by Fiona Pragoff.
       p. cm. -- (First step science)
    Includes bibliographical references and index.
    ISBN 0-8368-1114-3
    1. Apples--Juvenile literature. 2. Science--Juvenile literature.
  [1. Apples. 2. Science.] I. Oldfield, Wendy. II. Pragoff, Fiona, ill. III. Title. IV. Series.
  SB363.D38 1994
  634'.11--dc20   94-7107

This edition first published in 1994 by
Gareth Stevens Publishing
1555 North RiverCenter Drive, Suite 201
Milwaukee, Wisconsin 53212, USA

This edition © 1994 by Gareth Stevens, Inc. Original edition published in 1990 by A&C Black (Publishers) Ltd., 35 Bedford Row, London WC1R 4JH. © 1990 A&C Black (Publishers) Ltd. Photographs © 1990 by Fiona Pragoff except page 20, S. & O. Mathews. Additional end matter © 1994 by Gareth Stevens, Inc.

Series editor: Patricia Lantier-Sampon
Editorial assistants: Mary Dykstra, Diane Laska
Illustrations: Alex Ayliffe
Science consultant: Dr. Bryson Gore

Printed in the United States of America
1 2 3 4 5 6 7 8 9 99 98 97 96 95 94

At this time, Gareth Stevens, Inc., does not use 100 percent recycled paper, although the paper used in our books does contain about 30 percent recycled fiber. This decision was made after a careful study of current recycling procedures revealed their dubious environmental benefits. We will continue to explore recycling options.

First Step Science

My Apple

by Kay Davies and Wendy Oldfield
photographs by Fiona Pragoff

Gareth Stevens Publishing
MILWAUKEE

Look at all these apples!
What colors are they?

4

My apple is red and yellow.

5

At the top of my apple,
there's a stem.

The stem is tough, but it
bends easily.

I can hold my apple
by the stem.

It feels heavy.

My apple grew from
a flower.

At the bottom of my apple, I can see the dried-up parts of the flower.

9

The skin of my apple is smooth and hard.

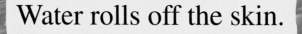
Water rolls off the skin.

If I drop my apple into the water, do you think it will float?

Nayo wants to know if she can hear the seeds rattle.

My apple tastes sweet and juicy.

I've eaten my apple.

I found six
seeds inside.

How many seeds did my
friends find inside their apples?

Nayo's apple is cut in half.

The seeds fit into little cases inside the core.

The white part soon turns brown!

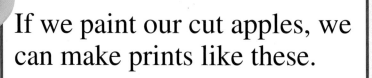

If we paint our cut apples, we can make prints like these.

If we plant the seeds in soil,
they may grow into tiny trees.

The apples on these trees are for cooking.

A cooking apple is bigger than my apple.

Cooking apples taste sour. But if we
cook them with honey and dried fruit. . .

they taste sweet.

How do you like to eat apples?

FOR MORE INFORMATION

Notes for Parents and Teachers

As you share this book with young readers, these notes may help you explain the scientific concepts behind the different activities.

pages 4, 5 Apple colors
Apples can be sorted into different groups according to the color of the skin. Apple color differs with the variety and ripeness of the apple.

pages 6, 7 Apple stems
The stem connects the apple to the tree and is the lifeline through which the apple receives food and water from the tree. The stem is strong enough to support the weight of the apple but flexible enough to withstand strong winds.

pages 8, 9 Apple flowers
Bees pollinate apple flowers and carry the yellow dust called pollen from one flower to another. If the pollen lands in the right place, a tiny apple starts to grow behind the petals. The flower withers, and the petals eventually drop off, leaving just a few dried-up parts of the flower behind.

pages 10, 11 Protective skin
The skin of an apple is firm, waxy, and waterproof to protect the soft flesh underneath. If the skin is bruised or broken, mold spores from the air can get inside to feed on the apple and make it decompose, or rot.

page 11 Floating apples

An apple is mostly made of water, and it floats in water. An apple is less dense than water.

pages 12, 14, 15, 16, 20, 21 Apple seeds

The number of seeds varies from apple to apple and variety to variety. When the seeds inside the apple are ripe, they dry out and become hard. Each seed contains the first roots and leaves of a tiny tree.

pages 13, 24, 25 Apple tasting

The soft, white part of an apple is a delicious fruit. Many animals eat apples and then disperse the seeds in their droppings.

page 17 Going brown

When the flesh of an apple is exposed to air, chemical changes take place that make the apple quickly turn brown.

pages 18, 19 Apple prints

You and your friends can make apple prints by cutting apples in half from top to bottom (this leaves a round hole in the center) or across the middle (this leaves a star-shaped hole).

pages 22, 23, 24, 25 Cooking apples

Have an adult help you make baked apples. First, remove the core of each apple and fill the space with dried fruit and honey or brown sugar. Then make a shallow cut around the middle of each apple. Place the apples in a shallow dish with a few table-spoons (milliliters) of water. Cook them at 400° F (200° C) for 3/4 to 1 hour until the insides of the apples are soft.

Things to Do

1. All sorts of seeds

Collect different fruits, such as plums, tomatoes, and grapes. Cut them open to look at the seeds inside. How many seeds are there inside each fruit? Do all the seeds have a hard coat? Are the seeds smooth, or do they have a rough surface pattern?

2. Apple tasting

See if you can find several varieties of apples and have an "apple tasting" with your friends. Ask an adult to help you cut each apple into small pieces. Give each friend one piece from each apple. Which variety does each friend like best?

3. Old apples

Find some old, bruised apples and watch them to see how they change as they decompose, or rot. Does any mold grow on these apples? If so, what color is the mold? How long does an apple take to completely decompose? Many animals like to eat all types of apples. Leave some of these apples outside for a treat.

4. Apple chemistry

Have an adult help you cut an apple in half from top to bottom. Pour a small amount of lemon juice over the cut side of one half of the apple. Do not pour juice over the other half. Leave both halves exposed to the air and watch what happens. Do you see a difference between the two halves? The lemon juice slows the chemical change that turns the apple brown.

Fun Facts about Apples

1. Apple trees grow on every continent of the Earth except Antarctica.

2. The apple tree probably originated in an area between the Black Sea and the Caspian Sea. Apples were a favorite fruit of the ancient Greeks and Romans.

3. Sunlight causes apples to change color. The light creates a chemical change in the apple sugar, causing a change in color.

4. The skin of the apple contains vitamins. Apples provide vitamins A and C, plus minerals like potassium.

5. Johnny Appleseed, whose real name was John Chapman (c. 1774-1847), was an American pioneer who spent his life planting apple seeds in the American Midwest.

6. Apple trees are members of the rose family. Other fruit trees belonging to the rose family are pear, peach, plum, and cherry.

7. The world record for the heaviest apple is three pounds and one ounce (1.4 kilograms). The longest unbroken apple peel on record was over 170 feet (52 meters)!

8. The world crop of apples averages about 32 million tons a year.

9. An apple tree uses the energy gathered by more than fifty leaves to grow just one apple.

Glossary

bend — to move, twist, or turn something so that it becomes curved or crooked.

cook — to prepare food for eating by using heat.

core — the center part of a fruit. Apples, pineapples, and pears have a core.

float — to rest or drift on top of a liquid or air.

grow — to become larger in size.

hard — solid; firm; difficult to bend or shape.

heavy — weighing a lot.

honey — a thick, sweet liquid that bees make from the nectar of flowers.

prints — patterns; designs.

rattle — to make a sharp, quick, noisy sound.

seeds — tiny parts of flowering plants. Seeds can be planted in soil to grow into new plants.

skin — the outer layer, or peel, of a fruit.

soil — the top layer of the Earth that is good for growing plants.

sour — having a sharp or tart taste.

stem — the stalk of a plant. A plant stem usually supports a leaf or a flower.

sweet —having a sugary taste.

tough — difficult to break apart; strong.

Places to Visit

Everything we do involves some basic scientific principles. Listed below are a few museums that offer a variety of scientific information and experiences. You may also be able to locate other museums in your area. Just remember: you don't always have to visit a museum to experience the wonders of science. Science is everywhere!

The Exploratorium
3601 Lyon Street
San Francisco, CA 94123

Museum of Science and Industry
57th Street and Lake Shore Drive
Chicago, IL 60637

The Smithsonian Institution
1000 Jefferson Drive SW
Washington, D.C. 20560

Ontario Science Center
770 Don Mills Road
Don Mills, Ontario
M3C 1T3

Royal British Columbia Museum
657 Belleville Street
Victoria, British Columbia
V8V 1X4

More Books to Read

All About Seeds
    Susan Kuchalla
    (Troll Associates)

An Apple a Day
    Dorothy H. Patent
    (E. P. Dutton)

Apple Tree
Barrie Watts
(Silver Burdett)

How Do Apples Grow?
Betsy Maestro
(Harper Trophy)

Apple Tree Through the Year
Claudia Schneipper
(Carolrhoda Books)

The Life and Times of the Apple
Charles Micucci
(Orchard Books)

Videotapes

A is for Apple (Handel Film Corporation)

All About Seeds (Troll)
Trees (Troll)

Index